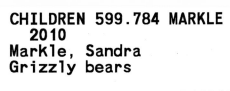

ANIMAL PREDATORS

Grizzly Bears

SANDRA MARKLE

LERNER PUBLICATIONS COMPANY / MINNEAPOLIS

THE ANIMAL WORLD IS FULL OF PREDATORS.

Predators are the hunters that find, catch, and eat other animals—their prey—in order to survive. Every environment has its chain of hunters. The smaller, slower, less able predators become prey for the bigger, faster, more cunning hunters. And everywhere, there are just a few kinds of predators at the top of the food chain. *In wilderness areas of Alaska and the northwestern part of Canada and the United States, one of these is the grizzly bear, also known as the grizzly.*

Why are grizzly bears one of the top predators? For one thing, the adults are big. By the time a male is twelve years old and fully grown, he may weigh close to 1,000 pounds (454 kilograms). The female weighs only half as much as a male. That's still big—too big for this wolverine to scare away. The wolverine growls fiercely as it backs off, leaving its meal to the grizzly.

Despite their massive size, grizzlies are fast. Adults can run for miles without stopping. For short distances, grizzlies can run as fast as 35 miles (55 kilometers) per hour—as fast as a horse can gallop.

Grizzly bears have keen senses that help them find and track prey. A grizzly sees about as well as a human, but it has better night vision. It also has excellent hearing. Its ears are on top of its head. Like satellite dishes, they can move to collect sound. Keenest of all its senses, though, is its sense of smell. A grizzly's world is shaped as much by what it smells as by what it sees and hears.

After an early autumn snow, this big male sniffed out a ground squirrel and dug it out of its tunnel. The ground squirrel tried to escape, but the grizzly grabbed it in its mouth. Grizzlies are omnivores, meaning they eat both animals and plants. Adults, especially big males, need to put on several hundred pounds (about 136 kg) each year to make it through the winter when they don't eat at all. To do that, they need to find fat-rich foods, like pine nuts, and all the animals they can catch, including small animals like ground squirrels and even army cutworm moths.

Another reason grizzly bears are successful top predators is they hunt only when they have the best chance of catching prey. Come October or November, when snow begins to pile up into deep drifts, the grizzly crawls into a natural cave or digs a den into a hillside. Snug inside its shelter, the bear hibernates, or rests in a kind of deep sleep.

Hibernation slows the bear's body functions way down. This way, the bear can make the most of its stored energy. Its heart rate slows from about fifty beats a minute to about eight to twelve. Its body temperature drops too, but only slightly. That's because its body uses its stored fat to stay warm. And even though the grizzly may wake from time to time, it doesn't eat, drink, or pass wastes until it emerges from its den. For males, that may be as early as late January. Females usually don't begin to emerge until late March.

Once awake after its long winter's sleep, a grizzly's first meal is likely to be a high-energy one, such as this bison, which struggled to find food over the winter and died in a blizzard.

Grizzly bears are also successful predators because they are clever. They choose a home range to settle into and learn the area well. This female's home is about 150 square miles (388 sq. km) of Yellowstone National Park. She's learned where and in what season certain foods are available in her range. She travels her range so that she is in the right area at the right time to eat those foods.

Not long out of her den, the female grizzly shuffles through the woods toward a meadow where elk grazed in past springs. When she picks up the scent of elk, she follows her nose through thick brush and between trees. Despite her bulky shape and big size, she pads along quietly, stepping over branches that could snap under her weight. Her coloring helps her blend into the background, so she manages to get close to an elk cow before being spotted.

The grizzly still isn't close enough to attack its prey, though, and the elk sprints away. Healthy and young, the elk is too fast for the grizzly to even bother chasing. Besides, from experience, the female grizzly knows at this time of year there is easier prey close by. She sniffs deeply and detects the scent of the elk cow's calf. She shuffles closer.

Suddenly, the calf explodes from its cover, and the bear chases after it. At first, the calf stays well ahead. Then the youngster comes to the edge of a stream and hesitates. It's a fatal mistake. The female grizzly catches up and snatches the elk calf out of the water.

The female grizzly
kills her prey with a
crushing neck bite.
Like other predators,
a grizzly has pointed
canine teeth. With these
teeth, she's able to easily
pierce her prey's skin. She
eats everything but the
hide and biggest bones.

Not many miles away, another female has recently left her den too. But she travels more slowly and doesn't chase after prey. She has two cubs, a little female and a little male, trying to keep up with her. She needs to stay close to them to defend them from predators, such as mountain lions, wolves, and other adult bears. She often stops to let her cubs nurse.

The cubs were born while the female grizzly was hibernating. Although she'd mated in July, the babies didn't start to develop until November when she was looking for a den site. After just two months, the female partly awakened to give birth to the cubs—each about the size of a soft-drink can. The newborn cubs were blind, toothless, and nearly hairless. They squealed as she licked them, removing the sticky birth fluid coating their bodies. This cleaning kept them from becoming too cold.

Then while the female grizzly slept again, each cub wriggled through her fur and curled up next to a nipple. The cubs slept, kept warm by their mother's body heat and breath, and often woke up to nurse. Because the grizzly bear's milk is even richer than whipping cream, the cubs grew quickly. By March, when they were ready to leave the den, they were cocker spaniel-sized, furry balls of energy.

Being naturally curious, the cubs watch what their mother eats and sample a little of these new foods. Although they have only baby teeth for their first year, those teeth are still strong enough to bite and chew. Sometimes the cubs try plants, like grasses.

Other times, they eat animals— even little ants that rush out when their mother lifts rocks or logs. An adult grizzly bear has claws about 3 inches (8 centimeters) long—about the length of an adult human's index finger. These claws are sturdy enough to lift rocks, dig in the ground, or tear apart rotten logs, especially when powered by swipes of a grizzly's strong paws. The strength for digging comes mainly from a mass of solid muscle on the grizzly's back, which forms a hump between its shoulders.

Sometimes, the cubs explore by themselves and nibble anything they can reach that smells interesting. This lets them test for new food sources as they exercise their developing muscles and grow stronger as well as bigger.

Wherever the female grizzly goes on her search for food, the cubs tag along. When one cub tires and squeals in complaint, the female lets it climb on her back to ride for a while.

While their mother stops to fish, the cubs wander away, exploring on their own. But they stay alert, and when one cub hears a sound, it quickly looks around. The youngster stretches tall to sniff the air and see farther, the way it has seen its mother do. What the cub discovers makes it bawl in fright.

A male grizzly is coming closer. To him, unattended bear cubs are just another kind of easy prey. The cubs take off running as their mother charges to their defense, roaring with her mouth open wide.

The cubs know what to do when in danger. They climb a tree. From high up among the branches, the youngsters watch the action below. Their mother continues her attack, and the male soon lumbers off. Even after the male grizzly leaves, though, the cubs stay put until their mother huffs and grunts, calling them down.

All through the summer, the grizzly cubs trail after their mother as she travels through her home range, searching for food. Everywhere they go, they discover new sights, sounds, smells, and tastes.

One afternoon in July, after waking from a nap, the female grizzly leads her family into a river to cool off and escape the buzzing, biting swarms of mosquitoes. While she soaks, the cubs wrestle, mimicking the male bears they can see farther downstream.

But those males aren't playing. They're battling over a female that's nearby. As the males face off, first one and then the other rears up to appear larger. Each male roars, flashing its mouthful of teeth. With powerful paw swipes, the fighting males draw blood. Ducking and bobbing, they try to bite each other's neck and head. The battle goes on until one of the males lowers its head and backs up, surrendering. The victor gets the chance to mate with the female.

This battle will be repeated by other males for other females, but not for the cubs' mother. She won't mate this year. Female grizzly bears don't mate while raising cubs.

Day after day, the bears continue to wander and feast on whatever they can find to eat. One day, the female picks up the odor of carrion, dead animal flesh. She tracks it, and her cubs follow along. But when she gets closer, she also smells wolves. Soon she sees the wolves feeding on an old moose carcass. She grunts, signaling her cubs to stay still. One wolf, catching the grizzly's scent, growls a warning to its family too.

The female grizzly charges, and the wolves rush to meet her attack. Although the bear is alone against the pack, her size and strength help her. When she drives the wolves away, she huffs to call her cubs to share her meal. The wolves stay close, waiting for a chance to eat the leftovers.

Day after day, the female bear and her cubs continue their traveling feast. In autumn, they feed nearly around the clock. Then one day, it starts to snow, and it keeps on snowing. When drifts pile up, the female grizzly chooses a den site and starts to dig. While she works, her fat, furry cubs play one more time before settling down to hibernate.

After the winter of hibernation, the cubs emerge in the spring of their second year. Once again, they travel with their mother, learning where to go to find food and what to eat. They also practice catching animal prey, like this ground squirrel, for themselves.

A little later in the spring, salmon and trout return to local rivers and streams. Each year, the fish come back to spawn, or reproduce. The mother bear shows the cubs how she catches fish, and the two-year-olds have plenty of chances to develop their fishing skills. Each time the young male catches a trout, he also learns to run away with his meal so he doesn't have to share it with his sister.

Grizzly bears are successful because the mother bears spend a lot of time raising their young. So when the female grizzly finally chases away her two-year-old cubs in late June, her offspring are able to feed themselves. They know what to eat, where to find food, and how to catch prey. They're also big enough so they no longer need her protection. In July, the female grizzly mates, and during the following winter, she gives birth to three cubs. Once again, she begins her task of raising another generation of hunters.

Looking Back

- Look back at the picture on page 7 to see a key grizzly bear feature, a shoulder hump. This mass of muscle helps power the grizzly's ability to use its paws to dig and strike. Take another look at page 31 to see a grizzly bear in action.

- Look at the book's cover and into the grizzly's mouth. Also look in the mirror at your own open mouth. How do the different shapes of the grizzly bear's teeth compare to yours? While yours are smaller and the pointed teeth aren't as long, the arrangement of the teeth is similar. Like you, a grizzly bear is equipped to be an omnivore, biting and chewing both plant matter and meat.

- What are some of the different things grizzly bears do with their long claws? To find out, take another look at these pages: 18, 19, 20, and 29.

- Compare the grizzly bear cubs on page 16 with those on page 27. What are some of the ways grizzly bear cubs change as they grow up?

Glossary

CANINE TEETH: pointed teeth used to tear meat

CARCASS: the body of a dead animal

CARNIVORE: an animal that eats only other animals

CARRION: the flesh of a dead animal

CUB: a young grizzly bear

DEN: a place where a grizzly bear finds shelter

HERBIVORE: an animal that eats only plants

HIBERNATE: a state in which an animal's heart rate slows and its body temperature lowers so much its food energy use is greatly reduced

HOME RANGE: the area within which a grizzly bear usually searches for food and for a mate. It's where a female raises her young.

OMNIVORE: an animal that eats both plants and animals, including insects, in order to survive

NURSE: to feed on milk from its mother's body

PREDATOR: an animal that hunts other animals

PREY: an animal that a predator catches to eat

SCAVENGER: an animal that feeds on dead animals

Further Information

Books

Chadwick, Douglas H., and Amy Shapira. *Growing Up Grizzly: The True Story of Baylee and Her Cubs.* Guilford, CT: Falcon, 2007. This is the unusual real-life story of a female grizzly who mothers a struggling two-year-old while raising her own three cubs.

Hoshino, Michio. *Hoshino's Alaska.* San Francisco: Chronicle, 2007. Take a tour of the Alaskan wilderness, home of grizzly bears, with a noted photographer. Also check out his *Grizzlies*, Chronicle, 1987; and *Grizzly Bear Family Book*, New York: North-South, 1997.

Sartore, Joel. *Face to Face with Grizzlies.* Washington, DC: National Geographic, 2007. Learn about a wildlife photographer's experiences observing grizzly bears in the wild.

Websites

The Bear Den
http://exn.ca/bears/bears.cfm?Show=Grizzlies
Dig into the facts and photos. Then take the Bear Quiz to discover even more.

Electronic Field Trip
http://www.windowsintowonderland.org/bears
Choose "Part 1: Bear Ecology" to take a virtual expedition into Yellowstone National Park and learn about the bears living there.

Wildcams: Grizzlies
http://www9.nationalgeographic.com/ngm/wildcamgrizzlies
From late June through early August, catch webcam action of grizzlies catching salmon on the McNeil River in Alaska.

Index

For Jean Craighead George, whose writing inspires me

The author would like to thank the following people for sharing their expertise and enthusiasm: Dr. Lance Craighead, Executive Director, Craighead Environmental Research Institute; and Dr. Christopher Servheen, Grizzly Bear Recovery Coordinator, United States Fish and Wildlife Service, University of Montana. The author would also like to express a special thank-you to Skip Jeffery for his help and support during the creative process.

Photo Acknowledgments

The images in this book are used with the permission of: © Michio Hoshino/Minden Pictures, p. 1; © Tom and Pat Leeson, pp. 3, 19; © Daniel J. Cox/NaturalExposures.com, pp. 4, 9, 35; © Mark Newman/Lonely Planet Images/Getty Images, p. 5; © Thomas D. Magnelsen, p. 7; © Norbert Rosing/National Geographic/Getty Images, pp. 11, 25; © Joe McDonald, pp. 13, 18, 20; © Tim Fitzharris/Minden Pictures, p. 14; © Kennan Ward/CORBIS, p. 15; © Leonard L. Rue/Bruce Coleman/Photoshot, p. 16; © Kathy Bushue/Stone/Getty Images, p. 21; © Art Wolfe/www.ArtWolfe.com, pp. 23, 29; © Eric Baccega/naturepl.com, pp. 24, 37; © E. & P. Bauer/zefa/CORBIS, p. 26; © Paul Souders/Riser/Getty Images, p. 27; © Eastcott Momatiuk/National Geographic/Getty Images, pp. 30, 31; © Juniors Bildarchiv/Photolibrary, p. 33; © W. Perry Conway/CORBIS, p. 34.
Cover: © Darrell Gulin/Stone/Getty Images.

Lerner Publications Company
A division of Lerner Publishing Group, Inc.
241 First Avenue North
Minneapolis, MN 55401 U.S.A.

Website address: www.lernerbooks.com

Websites listed in Further Reading are current at time of publication.

Library of Congress Cataloging-in-Publication Data

Markle, Sandra.
    Grizzly bears / by Sandra Markle.
        p.   cm. — (Animal predators)
    Includes bibliographical references and index.
    ISBN 978–1–58013–537–5 (lib. bdg. : alk. paper)
    1. Grizzly bear—Juvenile literature. I. Title.
QL737.C27M3448 2010
599.784—dc22   2008038120

Manufactured in the United States of America
1 2 3 4 5 6 – DP – 15 14 13 12 11 10